Contents

Prince William

THE FAIRYTALE PRINCE

Prince William attends a polo match in Santa Barbara, California, USA, 2011.

After the Princess of Wales' tragic death in 1997, Prince William walked behind his mother's coffin from the Mall to Westminster Abbey with his brother, father, grandfather and uncle.

Stats!

Name: Prince William Philip Arthur Louis

Royal title: His Royal Highness (HRH) Prince William, Duke of Cambridge, Earl of Strathearn and Baron Carrickfergus

Date of birth: 21 June 1982

Parents: The Prince of Wales and the late Diana, Princess of Wales.

Royal status: Second in line to the UK and Commonwealth thrones.

Education: Graduated from St Andrew's University in 2005, with a 2:1 honours in Geography.

Career: Prince William works as a Search and Rescue Pilot with the RAF.

Royal duties: As well as his military career, William carries out a number of official visits. He also supports many charities and organisations, including Centrepoint, the UK's homelessness charity. Instead of wedding presents, he and his wife, Catherine, asked guests to donate to their favourite charities.

Personal life: Prince William married Catherine Elizabeth Middleton on 29 April 2011 at Westminster Cathedral in London. It was a spectacular event, watched by two billion people around the world. The couple are now known as the Duke and Duchess of Cambridge. Their son, Prince George Alexander Louis, was born in July 2013.

KAY BARNHAM

WAYLAND

Published in 2013 by Wayland
Copyright © Wayland 2013

Wayland
338 Euston Road
London NW1 3BH

Wayland Australia
Level 17/207 Kent Street
Sydney, NSW 2000

Editor: Katie Woolley
Designer: D-R-ink

Picture Acknowledgements: The author and publisher would like to thank the following for allowing their pictures to be reproduced in this publication:

pp1 © EdStock/istock. pp2 © IAN LANGSDON/epa/Corbis. pp4 © Wirelmag/Getty Images. pp5 © waynehowes / Shutterstock.com. pp6 © Will Schneider/Rex Features. pp7 © John Stillwell/Pool/epa/Corbis. pp8 © IAN LANGSDON/epa/Corbis. pp9 © Getty Images. pp10 Getty Images Europe. pp11 © Sipa Press/Rex Features. pp12 © SIPHIWE SIBEKO/AP/Press Association Images. pp13 © AFP/Getty images. pp14 © David Fisher/Rex Features. pp15 © Maher Attar/Sygma/Corbis. pp16 © EdStock/istock. pp17 © Getty Images EUrope. pp18 © Getty Images. pp19 © Getty Images. pp20 © Getty Images. pp21 © IBL/Rex Features. pp22 Top. © Rex Features. Middle. © AHMED JADALLAH/Reuters/Corbis. Bottom xxxxx. pp23 Top. TOM RIVER/Rex Features. Middle. © EdStock/istock. Bottom. © Sankei via Getty Images

British Library Cataloguing in Publication Data
Barnham, Kay.
  Young royals. – (Celebrity secrets)
  1. Princes–Biography–Juvenile literature.
  2. Princesses–Biography–Juvenile literature.
  I. Title II. Series
  920'.008621-dc23

ISBN 978 0 7502 7878 2
Printed in China

10 9 8 7 6 5 4 3 2 1

Wayland is a division of Hachette Children's Books, an Hachette UK company.
www.hachette.co.uk

Life Story

Prince William has been famous since the day he was born. He went to Australia and New Zealand with his parents – the Prince and Princess of Wales – on his first royal tour when he was just nine months old. Even though he and his younger brother, Prince Harry, grew up in the media spotlight, their childhood wasn't all about being royal. Diana was determined that her sons should have a normal childhood. They went to theme parks, on holidays and enjoyed many of the things other children do.

The Duke and Duchess of Cambridge ride through the streets of London in a royal carriage on their wedding day.

An agreement between the Royal Family and the press meant that Prince William could go to university without being photographed by the paparazzi, in exchange for official photo opportunities.

He enjoyed three years of privacy at St Andrew's University in Scotland. While he was there, he met his future wife. Now, as well as doing his day job of flying search-and-rescue helicopters for the RAF, he and the Duchess of Cambridge go together on royal visits, departing on their first overseas tour to Canada and the USA just two months after their wedding. One day, they will be king and queen.

Questions and Answers

Q Have you grown used to being in the spotlight?

"I wouldn't really say I've grown used to it because I'm not really the attention-seeking type. So being in the centre of the spotlight is kind of awkward but it's something I've got to do and something I can adapt to."

Prince William, TV interview, November 2004

Q Diana, the Princess of Wales, was a massive iconic figure, the most famous of our age... is that intimidating?

"There's no pressure. Like Kate said, it is about carving your own future. No one is trying to fill my mother's shoes – what she did was fantastic. It's about making your own future and your own destiny and Kate will do a very good job of that."

Prince William, *press conference at St James's Palace, London*, November 2010

Prince Harry

THE SOLDIER PRINCE

Prince Harry attends a children's charity gala, Berlin, Germany 2010.

On his eighteenth birthday Queen Elizabeth II awarded Prince Harry his own coat of arms.

Stats!

Name: Prince Henry Charles Albert David

Royal title: HRH Prince Henry of Wales

Date of birth: 15 September 1984

Parents: The Prince of Wales and the late Diana, Princess of Wales.

Royal status: Third in line to the UK and Commonwealth thrones.

Education: Studied at Eton College, Windsor, where he passed A Levels in Art and Geography.

Career: Joined the Royal Military Academy at Sandhurst in 2005 and was commissioned as an army officer the following year. He served in Afghanistan for 10 weeks from December 2007 to February 2008 and then trained to be a helicopter pilot with the Army Air Corps. In 2013, he returned from Afghanistan after a four month tour as an Apache helicopter pilot.

Royal duties: Although he is focusing on his military career, Prince Harry is Patron to a number of charities. He and his brother Prince William created The Princes' Charities Forum, which supports charities for young people, the environment and the armed forces, among others.

Personal life: Chelsy Davy was Prince Harry's on-off girlfriend for five years. Most recently, he dated Florence Brudenell-Bruce – a descendant of the seventh Earl of Cardigan, and a very distant cousin of Harry himself – but they split up in August 2011. He has been dating model Cressida Bonas since July 2012.

Life Story

As the younger son of the Prince of Wales, Prince Harry has grown up knowing that he will probably never be king. While his elder brother has been the focus of the world's press, he has been allowed a little more privacy.

Questions and Answers

Q As a soldier, is being on the front line what it's all about?

"Yeah, this is what it is all about, what it's all about is being here with the guys rather than being in a room with a bunch of officers."

Prince Harry, *interview in Afghanistan*, the *Times*, January 2008

Q Do you get on well with your brother?

"I mean, ever since our mother died, obviously we were close, but he is the one person on this earth who I can actually really... you know, we can talk about anything."

Prince Harry, *interview to mark Prince Harry's twenty-first birthday*, September 2005

Prince Harry chose the army instead of university and went straight to Sandhurst after completing his A Levels. He has since risen through the ranks and, in 2011, he became a captain. Harry served on the front line in Afghanistan from December 2007 to February 2008, until the news was leaked and published in the Australian tabloid New Idea. Amid fears for his safety and that of his fellow soldiers, he was immediately withdrawn. He hopes to return to active service before the army leaves Afghanistan, though his Apache squadron is not due to return.

In April 2011, Prince Harry joined the Walking with the Wounded North Pole Expedition Team. He spent four days trekking across the Arctic with wounded servicemen to raise money for their charity. He also had a starring role at his brother's wedding as best man. He wore his Captain's uniform and his speech at that evening's party was reported to be 'hilarious'!

Prince Harry patrols through a deserted town in Afghanistan, January 2008.

Princesses Beatrice and Eugenie

THE ROYAL SISTERS

The princesses, Beatrice (left) and Eugenie (right), at the Duke and Duchess of Cambridge's wedding in April, 2011.

Stats!

Name: Princess Beatrice Elizabeth Mary; Princess Eugenie Victoria Helena.

Royal title: HRH Princess Beatrice of York; HRH Princess Eugenie of York.

Date of birth: 8 August 1988; 23 March 1990.

Parents: The Duke of York and Sarah, Duchess of York.

Royal status: Fifth and sixth in line to the UK and Commonwealth thrones.

Education: In 2011, Princess Beatrice graduated from Goldsmiths University, London, with a degree in History; Princess Eugenie studied for a degree in Art History, English Literature and Politics at Newcastle University.

Royal duties: Both princesses have official royal engagements, attend royal functions and support charities.

Personal lives: Beatrice has been seeing millionaire's son, Dave Clark, since 2006, when the couple were introduced to each other by Prince William! Princess Eugenie's boyfriend is barman, Jack Brooksbank.

Princess Beatrice was the first royal to be a movie star. She was an extra in The Young Victoria (2009) – a film about her great-great-great-great grandmother, Queen Victoria.

Life Story

Princess Beatrice and Princess Eugenie are the only two granddaughters of Queen Elizabeth II to be known as princesses. Their parents – Prince Andrew and Sarah, Duchess of York – divorced in 1996, but the family remains very close. The princesses spent a lot of time with both of their parents when they were growing up.

In 2010, Princess Beatrice became the first royal to run the London Marathon, when she raised money for several charities she supports. Princess Eugenie's first royal engagement was opening the Teenage Cancer Trust's unit in Leeds in 2009. Like her sister, she is seen at royal events and often photographed by the press. Eugenie is also a fan of reggae music, art and poetry.

When their cousin, Prince William, married in 2011, the princesses wore the most eye-catching hats of the day. Afterwards, Princess Beatrice sold her hat, which was designed by famous milliner Philip Treacy. It raised more than £80,000 for charity in an online auction.

Questions and Answers

Q Princess Beatrice, why did you decide to auction your hat?

A "I've been amazed by the amount of attention the hat has attracted. It's a wonderful opportunity to raise as much money as possible for two fantastic charities. I hope whoever wins the auction has as much fun with the hat as I have."

Princess Beatrice, the *Guardian,* May 2011

Q Princess Eugenie, do you and your sister get on?

A "We get on fantastically well, perhaps because we do and think different things… Like all sisters, we have silly arguments about unimportant stuff, but we do love each other to death."

Princess Eugenie, the *Telegraph*, March 2008

Charlotte Casiraghi

THE FILM STAR'S GRAND-DAUGHTER

Charlotte attends an international art exhibition in Venice in June, 2011.

In September 2011, Charlotte Casiraghi's status as a fashion icon was confirmed, when she appeared on the cover of the French edition of *Vogue*.

Stats!

Name: Charlotte Marie Pomeline Casiraghi

Royal title: None

Date of birth: 3 August 1986

Parents: Caroline, Princess of Monaco and the late Stefano Casiraghi.

Royal status: Fourth in line to the Monagesque throne.

Education: Is believed to have a degree in Philosophy from the University of Paris IV: Paris-Sorbonne.

Career: Charlotte is a competitive showjumper.

Royal duties: Charlotte undertakes a variety of royal engagements in Monaco, including presenting trophies for the Monaco Grand Prix. She also raises funds for the Princess Grace Foundation, which supports the arts.

Personal life: Notoriously private, Charlotte dated Alexander Dellal, who owns an art gallery in London for four years. She is now dating French actor, Gad Elmaleh.

Life Story

Charlotte Casiraghi might be the daughter of a princess of Monaco, but she is proud to be a Casiraghi. Her father was killed in a powerboat accident when she was just four years old. Afterwards, her mother – Princess Caroline – moved her young family to Provence in France in the hope of shielding them from the world's media. When the princess remarried in 1999, the family moved to Paris.

Questions and Answers

Q Is horse-riding your passion?

A "Yes, I started to ride horses when I was very young and it's a sport that I've been practising for a long time. It gives me a lot of pleasure."

Charlotte Casiraghi, *translated from a French TV interview in Monaco*

Q What's it like for amateur horse riders competing in the same tournament as professional riders?

A "Watching the top riders competing, you learn a lot from watching them… seeing such spectacular horses and incredible riders gives you the desire to go even further so I think it helps a lot of amateurs."

Charlotte Casiraghi, *TV interview in Monaco*, 2011

arlotte's grandmother s film star Grace Kelly, o won an Oscar for Best tress in *The Country rl* (1954).

Charlotte is fluent in French, Italian and English, and is believed to have a degree in Philosophy. She is also a keen showjumper. She has been riding horses since she was four and can often be found competing in prestigious events.

Many say that Charlotte inherited her beauty from her grandmother, Grace Kelly, who moved from Hollywood to Monaco in 1956 to marry Prince Rainier III. The legendary film star became a real-life fairytale princess.

As she spends more time in the public eye, Charlotte is becoming known as a style icon like her grandmother. When her uncle – Prince Albert II of Monaco – married Princess Charlene of Monaco in 2011, Charlotte was photographed wearing Chanel and YSL. Although she is a fan of haute couture, Charlotte supports eco-fashion, too.

Princess Sikhanyiso

THE MODERN PRINCESS

Princess Sikhanyiso wears traditional costume to attend a ceremony in Swaziland.

Stats!

Name: Sikhanyiso Dlamini

Royal title: Princess Sikhanyiso Dlamini of Swaziland

Date of birth: 1 September 1987

Parents: King MsWati III and LaMbikiza Sibonelo MngomeZulu.

Royal status: First in line to the throne of Swaziland.

Education: Went to school in the UK, before studying drama at Biola University in California, USA and then digital communication at Sydney University, Australia.

Royal duties: Princess Sikhanyiso takes part in traditional ceremonies in her native Swaziland.

Personal life: The princess is currently single.

Princess Sikhanyiso loves all sorts of music, but rap is her favourite. She's actually a rapper herself!

Life Story

The eldest daughter of King Mswati III, Princess Sikhanyiso has over twenty younger brothers and sisters. Her father is an absolute monarch, which means that he decides who runs the country's government, although he has to follow Swazi traditions, too.

The princess has spent many years studying overseas. She loves acting, dancing and singing, especially rap. But she has often been in trouble with the press because of behaviour that many regard as being too western. For example, the jeans she wears are not considered appropriate clothing for Swazi girls.

The princess' father, King Mswati III, currently has 14 wives and 23 children.

Not afraid to speak her mind, Princess Sikhanyiso also condemned the practice of polygamy – when a man is allowed to marry more than one woman. Some people are critical that she does not follow Swazi traditions and that she is extravagant when her country is poor.

However, Princess Sikhanyiso has never forgotten her roots. She regularly takes part in Swazi ceremonies, wearing traditional dress, and speaks fondly of her country in speeches abroad.

Questions and Answers

Q What's it like living in Australia?

A "Living here is very different. I have to do my own bed and my own cooking – I had to ask my aunty how to fry an egg!"

Princess Sikhanyiso, *Daily Telegraph, Australia,* June 2011

Q What do you hope to do in the future?

A "I still need to study more so that I can make my parents proud. I also want to contribute meaningfully to our beautiful country."

Princess Sikhanyiso, *Sowetan Live,* August 2010

Prince Azim

THE BILLIONAIRE PRINCE

Prince Azim attends London fashion week in 2011.

Stats!

Name: Prince Azim

Royal title: His Royal Highness Prince Haji 'Abdul 'Azim

Date of birth: 29 July 1982

Parents: Sultan Haji Hassanal Bolkiah and Pengiran Isteri Hajah Mariam.

Royal status: Third in line to the throne of Brunei.

Education: Went to schools in Brunei, Singapore, the UK and then studied Politics and International Relations at Oxford Brookes University in Oxford, UK.

Royal duties: Prince Azim is involved with a number of charities and carries out official engagements.

Personal life: The prince comes from a large family – he has 11 brothers and sisters.

It is rumoured that at one of his famously fabulous parties, Prince Azim spent £70,000 on flowers!

Life Story

Prince Azim's father is the Sultan of Brunei – one of the richest people in the world. After being educated around the globe, he started an officer training course at the Royal Military College at Sandhurst in the UK, but dropped out after just a few weeks.

Prince Azim is most famous for his fabulous parties. Diana Ross, Scarlett Johansson, Joan Collins, Kate Moss and the late Michael Jackson are just a few of the lucky guests.

Questions and Answers

Q Are you spoilt?

A "Yes, I'm spoilt! But I'm grateful to have what I have, and I like to share it. My mother was good in making us realise that material things aren't everything. If I had nothing tomorrow, I'd be able to live my life and still be happy and enjoy it, because I don't need all this gold. I just need e-mail and Twinkie rolls."

Prince Azim, *The Sunday Times*, April 2008

Q What exactly does a billionaire do all day?

A "Sometimes, I stay in bed all day and watch DVDs. Sometimes I write songs – lyrics. My friend has a studio, so I'll go to see him and put songs down, with him at the keyboard."

Prince Azim, *The Sunday Times*, April 2008

It is said that Prince Azim's guests go home with party bags filled with iPods, diamond jewellery and expensive face cream. The prince is a favourite with the world's press and is often photographed with supermodels and celebrities alike.

However, there is more to the prince than just parties. He spends much of his time holding fundraising events and supporting a range of charities, including the Make-A-Wish Foundation®, of which he is a patron.

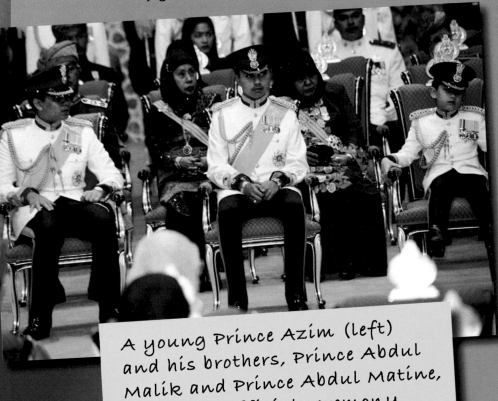

A young Prince Azim (left) and his brothers, Prince Abdul Malik and Prince Abdul Matine, attend an official ceremony, August 1998.

Princess Victoria

THE CROWN PRINCESS

Princess Victoria looks radiant on her wedding day, 19 June, 2010.

Stats!

Name: Princess Victoria Ingrid Alice Désirée

Royal title: Victoria, Crown Princess of Sweden, Duchess of Västergötland

Date of birth: 14 July 1977

Parents: King Carl XVI Gustaf of Sweden and Queen Silvia of Sweden.

Royal status: Heiress to the throne of Sweden.

Education: Went to school in Sweden and universities in France and the USA.

Royal duties: The princess is a very hard-working royal. She has travelled the world on official visits, while also supporting a number of charities and relief efforts. In 1997, the Crown Princess Victoria Fund was set up to support young people with disabilities or serious illnesses.

Personal life: Princess Victoria married Daniel Westling in 2010. In February 2012, the happy couple welcomed their first child, Princess Estelle Silvia Ewa Mary.

> **Every year, the Swedish people celebrate Victoria Day on the princess's birthday – 14 July. A special event is held, where there is live music and entertainment.**

Life Story

Princess Victoria is very highly educated. After school and university, she completed a number of post-graduate studies in the USA and in Sweden, including international peacekeeping, political science and conflict resolution. She puts her studies to good use by promoting Sweden and peacekeeping around the world.

There has always been a lot of media interest in the princess, who likes to keep her private life very private.

Prince Daniel (left) and Princess Victoria (centre) attend the FIS Nordic World Ski Championships 2011 in Oslo, Norway.

Daniel Westling was a gym owner who became the princess's personal trainer and then her boyfriend. Over the next eight years, the couple were spotted at sporting events, functions and parties. It was a very long romance and when it was announced that they would marry, all of Sweden were delighted.

The wedding in 2010 was one of the most expensive and lavish celebrations ever. For two weeks before the ceremony, Swedish people enjoyed free events held around the capital city. Hundreds of thousands of people lined the streets to watch the royal couple drive away from Stockholm's Cathedral in a horse-drawn carriage. Princess Victoria's husband is now known as Prince Daniel, Duke of Västergötland.

Questions and Answers

Q What do you see in Daniel?

A "It's a bit difficult to say … no, I'm only joking! He's a person with a really fantastic sense of humour… He's sociable and very friendly. He's someone I have great fun with. I'd say that Daniel and I laugh a lot and have a great deal in common. We have a lot of fun together."

Princess Victoria, *TV4 interview*, 17 May, 2010

Q Are you surprised that so many people turned up to see you on your birthday?

A "The weather is terrible, but it is fantastic that so many are still here. It is heart-warming and touching."

Princess Victoria, *interview*, 14 July 2011

Princess Sirivannavari

THE ARTISTIC PRINCESS

Princess Sirivannavari attends the Royal Wedding of Prince Albert II of Monaco to Princess Charlene of Monaco on 2 July, 2011.

Stats!

Name: Princess Sirivannavari

Royal title: Princess Sirivannavari Nariratana

Date of birth: 8 January 1987

Parents: Crown Prince Maha Vajiralongkorn and Yuvadhida Polpraserth.

Royal status: Fourth in line to the Thai throne.

Education: Studied fashion and textiles at Chulalongkorn University in Bangkok, Thailand.

Career: The princess is an artist as well as an internationally acclaimed fashion designer, who has worked with famous names such as Georgio Armarni and Karl Lagerfeld.

Royal duties: Princess Sirivannavari attends international events on behalf of her family.

Personal life: The princess is currently single.

The princess is sporty, too. She has competed at international level in badminton, winning a gold medal in the 2006 Southeast Asian Games.

Life Story

The daughter of Crown Prince Maha Vajiralongkorn, Princess Sirivannavari is a member of the richest royal family in the world. She isn't like other princesses. Princess Sirivannavari doesn't need to choose which fashion designer to follow – she's a designer herself!

After studying fashion and textiles at university, the princess continued her training at various different famous Parisian fashion houses.

Questions and Answers

Q **What are your feelings about photography?**

A "Photography isn't just about click and click… You need to carry a camera thinking what it is that you want to look at. You view that picture through your human lenses and keep it in your heart before using the camera to represent it."

Princess Sirivannavari, *Bangkok Post*, December 2010

Q **You're very artistic, aren't you?**

A "Sometimes, when I watch a movie, listen to a piece of music or see something I am unable to express, I turn it into an art work."

Princess Sirivannavari, *'How I see it' art exhibition*, November 2009

She achieved fame with her first collection at Paris Fashion Week in autumn 2007, which was inspired by traditional Thai clothing. She returned the following year to more success. Princess Sirivannavari's talents don't end there. She's also an accomplished photographer and an artist. In 2009, she displayed her drawings and paintings as part of an art exhibition in Bangkok, Thailand.

Often seen on the front row at Paris Fashion Week, Princess Sirivannavari is now spotted at major royal events around the world. She was photographed at Prince Albert II's wedding in Monaco in 2011, standing out from the crowds of royals in a traditional Thai outfit.

Princess Sirivannavari holds the relay torch at the National Stadium as part of the 15th Asian Games, Doha, in Bangkok, Thailand, November 2006.

19

Prince Carl Philip

THE PIN-UP PRINCE

Prince Carl Philip attends the wedding of the Prince of Monaco, July 2011.

In 2004 Prince Carl Philip had the honour of carrying the Olympic torch as it travelled through Stockholm on its way to Athens, Greece.

Stats!

Name: Prince Carl Philip

Royal title: Prince Carl Philip, Duke of Värmland

Date of birth: 13 May 1979

Parents: King Carl XVI Gustaf of Sweden and Queen Silvia of Sweden.

Royal status: Second in line to the throne of Sweden.

Education: Educated at a school in Sweden, then studied graphic design in the USA before attending the Swedish University of Agricultural Sciences in Alnarp.

Career: The Prince completed his military service in the Swedish Navy in 2000 and was then promoted through the ranks to lieutenant.

Royal duties: Prince Carl Philip represents his father, King Carl XVI Gustaf, and his sister, Princess Victoria (see pages 16-17), at official engagements when they are unable to attend.

Personal life: The prince has been seeing model and reality TV star Sophia Hellqvist since January 2010. Their romance was confirmed by the Swedish royal family in July 2010.

Life Story

Prince Carl Philip competes at the City Race arena in Gothenburg, Sweden, 9 June, 2009.

As the first son of King Carl XVI of Sweden, Prince Carl Philip was once the heir to the throne. But the year after he was born, Swedish law was changed. It was no longer the eldest son who would be the next monarch, but the eldest child, regardless of whether they were a prince or princess. This meant that the prince's elder sister, Princess Victoria, was now heir to the throne.

Without the pressures of being the next king, Prince Carl Philip is free to enjoy his spare time. He is a fan of motor racing and competes himself, winning his first race in 2010. The prince also loves football, swimming and skiing.

In 2003, he took part in the world's longest cross-country ski race – the Vasaloppet, which is a staggering 90km long!

Prince Carl Philip went out with public relations executive Emma Pernald for so long that they seemed guaranteed to marry. After a decade the couple split up, stunning the Swedish media. Now, the dashing prince is seeing reality TV star and model Sophia Hellqvist. Is Sophia set to become his princess…?

Questions and Answers

Q Why did you become interested in motor sport?

A "I think I got my interest in fast cars from my father… so I would sort of say that runs in the family."

Prince Carl-Philip

Q How do you feel after winning your first race?

A "Great! Everything clicked today, I made a really good start and … the feeling when I drove over the finishing line in the lead was fantastic."

Prince Carl-Philip, *interviewed after the GT Endurance Event, August 2010*

OTHER YOUNG ROYALS

Zara Phillips

Basic Information

Full name: Zara Anne Elizabeth Phillips, MBE.

Home: Born in London. Lives in Gloucestershire, UK.

Birthday: 15 May 1981

Royal Status: Thirteenth in line to the UK and Commonwealth thrones.

Background: Queen Elizabeth II's eldest granddaughter, Zara is a royal without a title.

Personal life: Zara married Mike Tindall, the captain of the England rugby team in Edinburgh on 30 July 2011. She is an excellent horse rider, winning the World Eventing Championship in 2006. She became the first royal Olympic medallist, winning silver at London 2012. Zara supports many charities, especially those linked with horse riding and children.

Sheikh Hamdan

Basic Information

Full name: Sheikh Hamdan bin Mohammed bin Rashid al Maktoum.

Home: Dubai.

Birthday: 13 November 1984

Royal Status: The Crown Prince of Dubai.

Background: In 2008, Sheikh Hamdan was made the Crown Prince of Dubai by his father, the Prime Minister of the United Arab Emirates and Dubai monarch.

Personal life: Sheikh Hamdan is the eldest son of 21 children. He is an accomplished equestrian, winning gold at the Asian games in 2006. He is also a famous poet, with a huge following in the Gulf States, writing under the name of Fazza.

Andrea Casiraghi

Basic Information

Full name: Andrea Albert Pierre Casiraghi.

Home: Born in Monte Carlo, Monaco. Lives in New York City.

Birthday: 8 June 1984

Royal Status: Andrea is currently second-in-line to the Monégasque throne after his mother, meaning that if the current reigning Prince Albert II were to die without legitimate children, then Casiraghi would adopt the surname Grimaldi and someday become the Prince of Monaco.

Background: After his father died, Andrea left Monaco and moved to France with his mother and two sisters. He later studied in North America. He is involved with a number of charities and is patron of the Motrice Foundation, which funds research into cerebral palsy.

Personal life: Andrea has been dating Tatiana Santa Domingo, a Colombian heiress, since 2004. Their son was born in March 2013. He is not afraid of a challenge. In May 2011, he dived out of a helicopter into the sea to raise money for a charity.

Prince Albert von Thurn und Taxis

Basic Information

Full name: Albert Maria Lamoral Miguel Johannes Gabriel, 12th Prince of Thurn und Taxis.

Home: Born in Regensburg, Bavaria, Germany. Currently lives in Germany.

Birthday: 24 June 1983

Royal Status: Albert is a prince in name only as the royal family was abolished in Germany in 1919.

Background: Prince Albert went to school in Rome and university in Edinburgh. Once the world's youngest billionaire, he owns large amounts of property and land.

Personal life: The prince is a huge fan of motorsport and races for a German team. He is currently single.

Princess Madeline

Basic Information

Full name: Madeline, Princess of Sweden.

Home: Madeline spends a lot of time in New York City, America, but her main home is in Stockholm, Sweden.

Birthday: 14 July 1977

Royal Status: Madeline is the youngest child and second daughter of King Carl XVI Gustaf and Queen Silvia of Sweden. Her official title is: Her Royal Highness Madeleine, Princess of Sweden, Duchess of Hälsingland and Gästrikland.

Background: Madeline was educated in Sweden and England and speaks many languages. She performs royal duties on behalf of her father and is the patron of a Swedish charity that makes wishes come true for children with serious illnesses.

Personal life: The princess loves skiing, theatre, dance, art and horse riding. In 2010 she came 3rd on a list - '10 Hottest Young Royals of 2010' – which was composed by the website PopCrunch. She married Christoper O'Neill, a New York banker, in June 2013.

Princess Tsuguko

Basic Information

Full name: Princess Tsuguko of Takamado.

Home: Born in Tokyo, Japan. She is currently studying in Shinjuku.

Birthday: 8 March 1986

Royal Status: Princess Tsuguko is a member of the Imperial House of Japan and the daughter of Prince Takamado and Princess Takamado.

Background: The princess graduated from the Gakushuin High School, and subsequently attended the University of Edinburgh in Scotland from 2004 to 2008, where she studied sociology and psychology. She is currently a student at Waseda University, School of International Liberal Studies.

Personal life: In 2008 she was included as 15th on the list of the '20 Hottest Young Royals' as compiled by Forbes Magazine. However, deeply private, the Princess is keen to keep her personal life out of the public eye.

More royals to look out for

Prince Wenzeslaus;

Sheikha Maitha bint Mohammed bin Rashid al Maktoum;

Princess Iman bint Al Hussein;

Prince Philippos, Princess Theodora;

Prince Amedeo;

Prince Félix Léopold Marie Guillaume;

Princess Sonam Dechen Wangchuck;

Pierre Casiraghi.

Index